SUPER CHICKEN!

SUPER CHICKEN!

THE BEST CHICKEN RECIPES

This edition published by Parragon Books Ltd in 2014
LOVE FOOD is an imprint of Parragon Books Ltd

Parragon Books Ltd
Chartist House
15–17 Trim Street
Bath BA1 1HA, UK
www.parragon.com/lovefood

ISBN: 978-1-4723-2986-8

Printed in China

New recipes written by Beverly Le Blanc
Introduction and incidental text written by Anne Sheasby
New photography by Clive Streeter
New home economy by Teresa Goldfinch
Additional design by Siân Williams
Internal illustrations by Nicola O'Byrne and Julie Ingham

Notes for the Reader
This book uses both metric and imperial measurements. Follow the same units of measurement throughout; do not mix metric and imperial. All spoon measurements are level: teaspoons are assumed to be 5 ml, and tablespoons are assumed to be 15 ml. Unless otherwise stated, milk is assumed to be full fat, eggs and individual vegetables are medium, and pepper is freshly ground black pepper. Unless otherwise stated, all root vegetables should be peeled prior to using.

Garnishes, decorations and serving suggestions are all optional and not necessarily included in the recipe ingredients or method. The times given are an approximate guide only. Preparation times differ according to the techniques used by different people and the cooking times may also vary from those given. Optional ingredients, variations or serving suggestions have not been included in the time calculations.

Picture acknowledgements
The publisher would like to thank the following for the permission to reproduce copyright material - cover illustration courtesy of iStock.

CONTENTS

PECKING ORDER

Chicken is the most readily available of all poultry and probably the most widely eaten too. Chicken is bred for its meat and eggs and can be obtained all year round. Depending on the type of chicken you buy and whether you buy a whole bird or chicken portions or pieces, it can also be an economical choice.

Chicken is versatile in cooking and is used in many different dishes across the world. It is easy to cook and is suitable for a wide variety of cooking methods including roasting, baking, pan-frying, stir-frying, deep-frying, grilling, griddling, barbecuing, poaching, steaming, pot-roasting, casseroling and braising.

Chicken breast meat is lean and pale with a fine texture and a delicate flavour. It tends to cook more quickly than the darker leg meat, which has a denser texture and is more flavourful. Small, tender chicken livers are delicately flavoured and are used to make dishes such as pâtés and terrines. The giblets (usually comprising the neck, gizzard, liver, heart and sometimes kidney) can be used to make stock.

Fresh or frozen raw chicken is available, sold either as whole, oven-ready birds or as chicken portions (including breasts on the bone, boneless breasts, mini fillets, whole legs, thighs, drumsticks and wings), diced chicken or minced chicken. Ready-prepared raw chicken such as marinated, seasoned or coated whole birds or portions, are also available for you to cook at home.

There are different types and breeds of chicken and most supermarkets and butchers, as well as other outlets, including farm shops and farmers' markets, offer a good range of chicken to buy. If you can, choose free-range or organic birds as they will have had a better upbringing to higher welfare standards, they are a more ethical and healthy choice and their flavour is often superior, but they are also more expensive.

Ideally, buy the best quality chicken that you can afford from a trusted supplier (who should also be able to tell you where the chicken came from and how it was reared). Intensively reared chickens are cheaper, but the quality, flavour and texture of the meat can be affected by the way the birds are bred or factory-farmed and are usually inferior as a consequence of this.

Chicken is an excellent source of protein and provides some vitamins and minerals, including B vitamins and selenium. Chicken is also low in fat and is lower in saturated fat than many other meats, especially when the skin is removed. The skin can be left on during cooking to help keep the chicken moist and add flavour, then you can remove it before serving, if you like.

STARTERS, SNACKS & SIDES

CHICKEN CROSTINI

SERVES: 4 **PREP TIME: 15 MINS** **COOK TIME: 10 MINS**

INGREDIENTS

12 slices of French bread or rustic bread

4 tbsp olive oil

2 garlic cloves, chopped

2 tbsp fresh oregano, finely chopped, plus extra to garnish

100 g/3½ oz cold roast chicken, cut into thin slices

4 tomatoes, sliced

12 thin slices of goat's cheese

12 black olives, stoned and chopped

salt and pepper

1. Preheat the oven to 180°C/350°F/Gas Mark 4 and the grill to medium. Put the bread under the preheated grill and lightly toast on both sides.

2. Meanwhile, pour the oil into a bowl and add the garlic and oregano. Season to taste with salt and pepper and mix well. Remove the toasted bread slices from the grill and spoon a little of the oil mixture on one side only.

3. Place the bread slices, oiled sides up, on a baking sheet. Put some of the sliced chicken on top of each one, followed by a slice of tomato. Divide the slices of goat's cheese among them, then top with the olives.

4. Drizzle over the remaining oil mixture and transfer to the preheated oven. Bake for about 5 minutes, or until the cheese is golden and starting to melt. Garnish with oregano and serve immediately.

CHICKEN SALAD CUPS

Chicken salad is great for picnics and is easily assembled. Here the salad is served in dainty toast cups, but it can also be spread on slices of soft bread and turned into a sandwich.

MAKES: 20 FILLED TOAST CUPS

PREP TIME: 20–25 MINS

COOK TIME: 10–15 MINS PLUS COOLING

INGREDIENTS

1 loaf thinly sliced white bread

unsalted butter or margarine, softened

225 g/8 oz cooked chicken, finely chopped

115 g/4 oz celery, finely chopped

35 g/1¼ oz toasted pecans, finely chopped

1 tsp honey mustard

1 tsp lemon juice

mayonnaise

salt and pepper

1. Preheat the oven to 160°C/325 °F/Gas Mark 3. Roll the bread slices flat with a rolling pin. Lightly butter one side of each slice of bread. Cut a round from each slice, using a small cookie or biscuit cutter. Press the rounds into ramekins, buttered side up. Bake in the preheated oven for 10–15 minutes, or until lightly browned. Remove from the ramekins and cool completely.

2. Combine the chicken, celery, pecans, honey mustard, and lemon juice in a bowl stirring gently. Add enough mayonnaise to moisten the chicken mixture. Season to taste with salt and pepper. Fill the toast cups with the chicken mixture and serve immediately.

CRISPY CHICKEN & HAM CROQUETTES

These croquettes make a great appetizer or a snack at any time of day. Serve them with aïoli or another dipping sauce of your choice.

MAKES: 8

PREP TIME: 20 MINS PLUS CHILLING

COOK TIME: 20–25 MINS

INGREDIENTS

4 tbsp olive oil

4 tbsp plain flour

200 ml/7 fl oz milk

115 g/4 oz cooked chicken, minced

55 g/2 oz Serrano ham, very finely chopped

1 tbsp chopped fresh flat-leaf parsley

small pinch of freshly grated nutmeg

1 egg, beaten

55 g/2 oz day-old white breadcrumbs

sunflower oil, for deep-frying

salt and pepper

aïoli, to serve

1. Heat the olive oil in a saucepan over a medium heat. Stir in the flour to form a paste and cook gently for 1 minute, stirring constantly.

2. Remove the pan from the heat and gradually stir in the milk until smooth. Return to the heat and slowly bring to the boil, stirring constantly, until the mixture boils and begins to thicken.

3. Remove the pan from the heat, add the chicken and beat until the mixture is smooth. Add the ham, parsley and nutmeg and mix well. Season to taste with salt and pepper.

4. Spread the chicken mixture in a dish and leave for 30 minutes until cool, then cover and chill in the refrigerator for 2–3 hours or overnight.

5. Divide the chicken mixture into eight portions. Use wet hands to form each portion into a cylindrical shape.

6. Pour the beaten egg onto a plate and put the breadcrumbs on a separate plate. Dip the croquettes, one at a time, in the beaten egg, then roll in the breadcrumbs to coat. Chill in the refrigerator for at least 1 hour.

7. Heat enough sunflower oil for deep-frying in a large saucepan or deep-fat fryer to 180–190°C/350–375°F, or until a cube of bread browns in 30 seconds. Add the croquettes, and deep-fry for 5–10 minutes, or until golden brown and crisp.

8. Remove the croquettes with a slotted spoon and drain well on kitchen paper.

9. Serve piping hot, accompanied by aïoli for dipping.

QUICK CHICKEN NACHOS

Nachos are always a big hit with all the family! The addition of chicken to this favourite makes for a tasty twist on the classic version using refried beans.

SERVES: 4   **PREP TIME: 10 MINS**   **COOK TIME: 10–15 MINS**

INGREDIENTS

100 g/3½ oz salted tortilla chips

150 g/5½ oz cooked chicken, shredded

85 g/3 oz Cheddar cheese, grated

pepper

6 tbsp tomato salsa, to serve

6 tbsp soured cream, to serve

1. Place a large piece of double-thickness aluminium foil in the base of a non-stick frying pan and place the pan over a medium–high heat.

2. Place the tortilla chips in a single layer on the foil. Scatter over the chicken and cheese. Cover the pan either with a lid or with some foil.

3. Cook the nachos for about 10–15 minutes until the cheese is just molten (check by opening up the foil regularly).

4. Season to taste with pepper and serve the nachos with the salsa and soured cream liberally spooned over.

STICKY GINGER & SOY CHICKEN WINGS

It is always a particularly gratifying experience eating food with your fingers, and these sticky, sweet wings are a real treat.

SERVES: 4　　　**PREP TIME: 15 MINS PLUS MARINATING**　　　**COOK TIME: 12–15 MINS**

INGREDIENTS

12 chicken wings
2 garlic cloves, crushed
2.5-cm/1-inch piece fresh ginger, peeled and chopped
2 tbsp dark soy sauce
2 tbsp lime juice
1 tbsp clear honey
1 tsp chilli sauce
2 tsp sesame oil
lime wedges, to serve

1. Tuck the pointed tip of each wing under the thicker end to make a neat triangle.

2. Mix together the garlic, ginger, soy sauce, lime juice, honey, chilli sauce and oil.

3. Spoon the mixture over the chicken and turn to coat evenly. Cover and marinate for several hours or overnight.

4. Preheat the grill to hot. Cook the wings on a foil-lined grill pan for 12–15 minutes, or until the juices run clear when a skewer is inserted into the thickest part of the meat, basting often with the marinade.

5. Serve hot, with lime wedges.

HERO TIPS

If you are serving these delicious wings for guests make sure that you have plenty of serviettes and a finger bowl for cleaning sticky fingers.

CHICKEN WINGS

SERVES: 4   **PREP TIME: 40-45 MINS   COOK TIME: 20-25 MINS**

INGREDIENTS

12 chicken wings
1 egg
4 tbsp milk
70 g/2½ oz plain flour
1 tsp paprika
225 g/8 oz breadcrumbs
55 g/2 oz butter
salt and pepper

1. Preheat the oven to 220°C/425°F/Gas Mark 7. Separate each chicken wing into three pieces, discarding the bony tip. Beat the egg with the milk in a shallow dish.

2. Combine the flour, paprika, and salt and pepper to taste in a shallow dish. Place the breadcrumbs in another dish. Dip the chicken in the egg mixture, drain and roll in the flour.

3. Shake off any excess, then roll the chicken wings in the breadcrumbs, gently pressing them onto the surface and shaking off any excess.

4. Put the butter in a wide, shallow roasting tin and place in the preheated oven to melt.

5. Place the chicken in the tin skin side down.

6. Bake for 10 minutes on each side. To check that the wings are cooked through, cut into the middle to check that there are no remaining traces of pink or red.

7. Transfer the chicken to a serving platter and serve.

BARBECUE-GLAZED DRUMSTICKS

SERVES: 6

**PREP TIME: 15 MINS
PLUS MARINATING**

COOK TIME: 1 HR

INGREDIENTS

12 chicken drumsticks,
about 1.6 kg/3 lb 8 oz
225 ml/8 fl oz barbecue sauce
1 tbsp soft light brown sugar
1 tbsp cider vinegar
1 tsp salt
½ tsp pepper
½ tsp hot pepper sauce
vegetable oil, for brushing
salad, to serve

1. Using a sharp knife, make two slashes, about 2.5 cm/1 inch apart, into the thickest part of the drumsticks, cutting to the bone. Put the drumsticks into a large, sealable polythene freezer bag.

2. Mix together 4 tablespoons of the barbecue sauce, the sugar, vinegar, salt, pepper and hot pepper sauce in a small bowl. Pour the mixture into the bag, press out most of the air and seal tightly. Shake the bag gently to distribute the sauce evenly and leave to marinate in the refrigerator for at least 4 hours.

3. Preheat the oven to 200°C/400°F/Gas Mark 6. Line a baking sheet with foil and brush lightly with oil.

4. Using tongs, transfer the drumsticks to the prepared baking sheet. Discard the marinade. Brush both sides of the drumsticks with some of the remaining barbecue sauce.

5. Bake for 15 minutes, then remove from the oven and brush generously with more barbecue sauce. Return to the oven and repeat this process three more times for a total cooking time of 1 hour or until the chicken is tender and the juices run clear when a skewer is inserted into the thickest part of the meat. Serve with salad.

COUNT YOUR CHICKENS!

An average-size chicken weighs about 1.5 kg/3 lb 5 oz and will feed a family of four with some leftovers for the next day. You can also make your own stock from the raw or cooked chicken carcass (see pages 50-51) to be used fresh (or frozen for later use) in recipes such as soups, risottos, casseroles or stews. If you can spare a little extra time and effort, then it is usually much more economical to buy a whole chicken and joint it yourself, than to buy chicken breasts, thighs and leg joints.

JOINTING A CHICKEN

When jointing a chicken, it can either be cut into four pieces (2 leg and 2 breast joints) or eight pieces (2 thigh, 2 drumstick, 2 breast and 2 wing joints).

• Before jointing, remove and discard any trussing string. Using a large, sharp knife, remove and discard the wishbone. Using poultry shears or a sharp knife, pull out each wing joint, then cut off the wing tips (the wing tips can be used to make stock, along with the raw carcass, if you like).

• Position the chicken, breast-side up, on a chopping board, then cut down through the skin on one side of the chicken between the leg and the body, as close to the leg as possible. Bend the leg back (away from the body) as far as you can and twist sharply until you dislocate the ball and socket joint between the thigh bone and ribcage, then cut the leg away to release it from the body. Repeat the process with the other leg.

At this stage (if you want eight joints), each leg can be divided into thigh and drumstick. To do this, lay each leg joint out on the chopping board, find the joint connecting the drumstick to the thigh and cut down through it to separate the leg into thigh and drumstick. Trim off the top end of the drumstick too (these trimmings can also be used to make stock). Repeat the process with the other leg.

• To remove each breast with the bone in, cut along one side of the length of the breastbone from neck to tail using a sharp knife, then cut down as close to the bone as you can, following the contour of the breast meat. Using sharp kitchen scissors or poultry shears, cut through the rib bones that join the breast onto the breastbone, then snip along the fat line on the other side of the breast (around the side of the breast), cutting through the meat and

skin to remove the breast from the body. Trim away any unwanted flaps of skin or fat. Repeat the process on the other side.

At this stage (if you want eight joints), each breast joint can be cut diagonally in half, so one portion has a wing joint with some breast meat and the other one is just breast meat.

• To remove each breast from the bone, using a sharp knife, gently cut and ease the flesh away from the ribs, cutting down between the flesh and ribs of one breast and separating the meat from the ribs, following the shape of the ribcage/breastbone underneath the fillet. Cut the fillet away neatly. Repeat the process on the other breast.

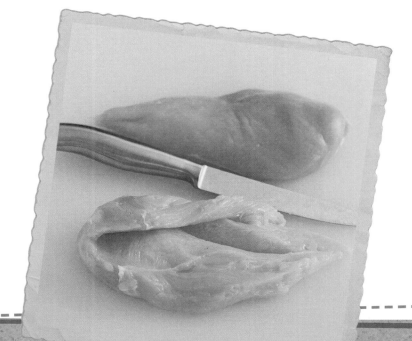

CHICKEN-LOADED POTATO SKINS

SERVES: 4   **PREP TIME: 15 MINS**   **COOK TIME: 15–20 MINS**

INGREDIENTS

4 jacket potatoes, halved lengthways

2 tbsp sunflower oil, plus extra for oiling

1 onion, finely chopped

2 tbsp plain flour

freshly grated nutmeg, to taste

300 ml/10 fl oz milk

200 g/7 oz boneless, skinless cooked chicken, diced

200 g/7 oz cooked ham, diced

2 sun-dried tomatoes in oil, drained and thinly sliced

2 tbsp chopped fresh flat-leaf parsley, plus extra to garnish

125 g/4½ oz mozzarella cheese, drained and grated

salt and pepper

1. Preheat the grill to high and position a rack 13 cm/5 inches from the heat.

2. Scoop out the potato flesh, leaving a 5-mm/¼-inch shell. (The flesh can be used in other recipes.) Rub the potato skins with oil, then season with salt and pepper.

3. Place the skins on a baking sheet, cut side up, place under the grill and cook for 5 minutes. Turn and cook for a further 3–5 minutes until crisp. Remove from the heat, but do not switch off the grill.

4. Meanwhile, heat the oil in a saucepan. Add the onion and fry for 2–3 minutes until soft. Add the flour and nutmeg and stir for 2 minutes, then slowly stir in the milk. Bring to the boil, then reduce the heat and simmer for 2 minutes.

5. Stir in the chicken, ham, tomatoes and parsley and season to taste with salt and pepper.

6. Divide the mixture between the potato skins and sprinkle with the cheese. Return to the grill and cook for 4–5 minutes, or until the cheese is bubbling. Sprinkle with flat-leaf parsley and serve.

CHICKEN BALLS WITH DIPPING SAUCE

SERVES: 4   **PREP TIME: 20 MINS**   **COOK TIME: 10–15 MINS**

INGREDIENTS

2 large skinless, boneless chicken breasts

3 tbsp vegetable oil

2 shallots, finely chopped

½ celery stick, finely chopped

1 garlic clove, crushed

2 tbsp light soy sauce

1 small egg, lightly beaten

1 bunch of spring onions

salt and pepper

DIPPING SAUCE

3 tbsp dark soy sauce

1 tbsp rice wine

1 tsp sesame seeds

1. Cut the chicken into 2-cm/¾-inch pieces. Heat half of the oil in a frying pan and stir-fry the chicken over a high heat for 2–3 minutes, until golden. Remove from the pan with a slotted spoon and set aside.

2. Add the shallots, celery and garlic to the pan and stir-fry for 1–2 minutes, until softened.

3. Place the chicken and the shallot mixture in a food processor and process until finely minced. Add 1 tablespoon of the light soy sauce and just enough of the egg to make a fairly firm mixture. Season to taste with salt and pepper.

4. To make the dipping sauce, mix together the dark soy sauce, rice wine and sesame seeds in a small serving bowl and set aside.

5. Shape the chicken mixture into 16 walnut-sized balls. Heat the remaining oil in the pan and stir-fry the chicken balls in small batches for 4–5 minutes, until golden brown. Drain on kitchen paper.

6. Add the spring onions to the pan and stir-fry for 1–2 minutes, until they begin to soften, then stir in the remaining light soy sauce. Serve the chicken balls with the stir-fried spring onions and the dipping sauce.

CHICKEN SATAY SKEWERS

SERVES: 4

PREP TIME: 15 MINS PLUS SOAKING & MARINATING

COOK TIME: 10 MINS

INGREDIENTS

4 skinless, boneless chicken breasts, about 115 g/4 oz each, cut into 2-cm/¾-inch cubes

4 tbsp soy sauce

1 tbsp cornflour

2 garlic cloves, finely chopped

2.5-cm/1-inch piece fresh ginger, peeled and finely chopped

1 cucumber, diced, to serve

PEANUT SAUCE

2 tbsp groundnut oil or vegetable oil

½ onion, finely chopped

1 garlic clove, finely chopped

4 tbsp crunchy peanut butter

4–5 tbsp water

½ tsp chilli powder

1. Put the chicken cubes in a shallow dish. Mix the soy sauce, cornflour, garlic and ginger together in a small bowl and pour over the chicken. Cover and leave to marinate in the refrigerator for at least 2 hours.

2. Meanwhile, soak 12 wooden skewers in cold water for at least 30 minutes. Preheat the grill and thread the chicken pieces onto the wooden skewers. Transfer the skewers to a griddle pan and cook under a preheated grill for 3–4 minutes. Turn the skewers over and cook for a further 3–4 minutes or until cooked through. To check the chicken cubes are cooked through, cut into the middle to check that there are no remaining traces of pink or red.

3. Meanwhile, to make the sauce, heat the oil in a saucepan, add the onion and garlic and cook over a medium heat, stirring frequently, for 3–4 minutes until softened. Add the peanut butter, water and chilli powder and simmer for 2–3 minutes until softened and thinned. Serve the skewers immediately with the warm sauce and cucumber.

SAUTÉED CHICKEN & GARLIC

This is a gorgeous dish and works particularly well with some fresh crusty bread to help mop up all of the delicious juices.

SERVES: 8   **PREP TIME: 10 MINS**   **COOK TIME: 25–30 MINS**

INGREDIENTS

8 skin-on chicken thighs, boned if available

hot or sweet smoked paprika, to taste

4 tbsp olive oil

10 garlic cloves, sliced

125 ml/4 fl oz dry white wine

1 bay leaf

salt

fresh flat-leaf parsley, chopped, to garnish

crusty bread, to serve (optional)

1. If necessary, halve the chicken thighs and remove the bones, then cut the flesh into bite-sized pieces, leaving the skin on. Season with paprika.

2. Heat the oil in a large frying pan or a flameproof casserole, add the garlic slices and cook over a medium heat, stirring frequently, for 1 minute until golden brown. Remove with a slotted spoon and drain on kitchen paper.

3. Add the chicken pieces to the pan and cook, turning occasionally, for 10 minutes, or until tender and golden brown on all sides. Add the wine and bay leaf and bring to the boil. Reduce the heat and simmer, stirring occasionally, for 10 minutes, or until most of the liquid has evaporated. Cut into the middle of the chicken to check there are no remaining traces of pink or red. Remove and discard the bay leaf and season to taste with salt.

4. Transfer the chicken to a warmed serving dish and sprinkle over the reserved garlic slices. Scatter with chopped parsley to garnish and serve with chunks of crusty bread to mop up the juices, if desired.

CHICKEN ROLLS WITH OLIVES

These rolls look impressive but use few ingredients and take little time to prepare and cook. Serve to friends at a dinner party to create a real wow factor.

SERVES: 6-8　　　**PREP TIME: 15-20 MINS**　　**COOK TIME: 25-30 MINS**

INGREDIENTS

115 g/4 oz black olives in oil, drained and 2 tbsp oil reserved

140 g/5 oz butter, softened

4 tbsp chopped fresh parsley

4 skinless, boneless chicken breasts

1. Preheat the oven to 200°C/400°F/Gas Mark 6. Stone and finely chop the olives. Mix together the olives, butter and parsley in a bowl. Place the chicken breasts between two sheets of clingfilm and gently beat with a meat mallet or the side of a rolling pin.

2. Spread the olive and parsley butter over one side of each flattened chicken breast and roll up.

3. Secure with wooden cocktail sticks or tie with kitchen string.

4. Place the chicken rolls in an ovenproof dish. Drizzle over the reserved oil from the olives and bake in the preheated oven for 25–30 minutes. Cut into the middle of the chicken to check there are no remaining traces of pink or red.

5. Transfer the chicken rolls to a chopping board, discard the cocktail sticks or string and slice with a sharp knife.

6. Transfer to a warmed serving plate and serve immediately.

CHICKEN PÂTÉ

SERVES: 4

**PREP TIME: 20–25 MINS   COOK TIME: 10–15 MINS
PLUS CHILLING**

INGREDIENTS

140 g/5 oz butter
1 onion, finely chopped
1 garlic clove, finely chopped
250 g/9 oz chicken livers
½ tsp Dijon mustard
2 tbsp brandy (optional)
salt and pepper
brown toast fingers and
green olives, to serve

CLARIFIED BUTTER

115 g/4 oz lightly salted
butter

1. Melt half the butter in a large frying pan over a medium heat and cook the onion for 3–4 minutes until soft and transparent. Add the garlic and continue to cook for a further 2 minutes.

2. Check the chicken livers and remove any discoloured parts using a pair of scissors. Add the livers to the frying pan and cook over quite a high heat for 5–6 minutes until they are brown in colour.

3. Season well with salt and pepper and add the mustard and brandy, if using.

4. Process the pâté in a blender or food processor until smooth. Add the remaining butter cut into small pieces and process again until creamy.

5. Press the pâté into a serving dish or 4 small ramekins, smooth over the surface and cover with clingfilm. If the pâté is to be kept for more than 2 days, you could cover the surface with a little clarified butter. In a clean saucepan, heat the butter until it melts, then continue heating for a few moments until it stops bubbling. Allow the sediment to settle and carefully pour the clarified butter over the pâté.

6. Chill in the refrigerator until ready to serve, accompanied by toast fingers and green olives.

PARMESAN CHICKEN TENDERS

The great things about these tender strips of baked cheesy chicken is that they are as popular with adults as with children, and they are equally good eaten hot or cold.

SERVES: 4

PREP TIME: 20 MINS PLUS MARINATING

COOK TIME: 20–25 MINS

INGREDIENTS

4 boneless, skinless chicken breasts, each about 175 g/ 6 oz, cut across the grain into 1-cm/½-inch wide strips

55 g/2 oz panko breadcrumbs, finely crushed

55 g/2 oz freshly grated Parmesan cheese

3 tbsp self-raising flour

¼ tsp paprika, or to taste

olive oil or vegetable oil spray

cooked green vegetables, to serve

MARINADE

150 ml/5 fl oz buttermilk

1 egg, lightly beaten

salt and pepper

cooked green vegetables, to serve

1. To make the marinade, combine the buttermilk and egg in a large bowl and season to taste with salt and pepper. Stir in the chicken strips, then cover the bowl and marinate in the refrigerator for 2–4 hours.

2. When ready to cook, preheat the oven to 190°C/375°F/Gas Mark 5 and line two baking sheets with baking paper. Toss together the breadcrumbs, cheese, flour and paprika in a wide bowl.

3. Remove a piece of chicken from the marinade, allowing the excess to drip back into the bowl. Place in the breadcrumb mixture and toss until coated, then transfer to the prepared baking sheet. Continue until all the chicken pieces are coated. Lightly spray each piece with oil.

4. Bake in the preheated oven for 20–25 minutes until golden brown. Cut into the middle of the chicken to check there are no remaining traces of pink or red. Serve with vegetables.

LOVELY LUNCHES

CHICKEN CAESAR SALAD

SERVES: 4   PREP TIME: 20 MINS   COOK TIME: 20 MINS

INGREDIENTS

3 tbsp sunflower oil

2 thick slices of white bread, cubed

3 skinless, boneless chicken breasts, about 140 g/5 oz each

2 small heads of cos lettuce, roughly chopped

2 tbsp Parmesan cheese shavings

salt and pepper

DRESSING

1 garlic clove, crushed

2 canned anchovy fillets, drained and finely chopped

5 tbsp light olive oil

2 tbsp white wine vinegar

2 tbsp mayonnaise

2 tbsp freshly grated Parmesan cheese

salt and pepper

1. Preheat the oven to 200°C/400°F/Gas Mark 6. Place 2 tablespoons of the sunflower oil in a bowl, add the bread and toss to coat in the oil. Spread out on a baking sheet, season well with salt and pepper and bake in the preheated oven for 10 minutes, until crisp and golden brown.

2. Meanwhile, brush the chicken breasts with the remaining sunflower oil and season to taste with salt and pepper. Cook on a preheated cast-iron skillet for 8–10 minutes on each side, until the chicken is tender and the juices run clear when a skewer is inserted into the thickest part of the meat.

3. To make the dressing, place all the ingredients in a small bowl and mix thoroughly until smooth and creamy.

4. Slice the hot cooked chicken and toss lightly with the lettuce and croûtons. Divide the salad among four serving bowls and drizzle over the dressing. Scatter over the Parmesan cheese shavings and serve immediately.

CHICKEN & PESTO SALAD

SERVES: 4

PREP TIME: 15 MINS PLUS COOLING & CHILLING

COOK TIME: 20–25 MINS

INGREDIENTS

4 large chicken thighs

sunflower oil or olive oil, for brushing

200 g/7 oz dried fusilli pasta

200 g/7 oz fine French beans, chopped

300 g/10½ oz ready-made pesto, plus extra if needed

2 large tomatoes, sliced

salt and pepper

fresh basil leaves, to garnish

1. Preheat the grill to medium–high and position the grill rack about 7.5 cm/3 inches below the heat. Brush the chicken thighs with oil and season to taste with salt and pepper. Brush the rack with a little oil, add the chicken thighs, skin-side up, and cook for 20–25 minutes, or until the chicken is cooked through and the juices run clear when a skewer is inserted into the thickest part of the meat. Remove from the heat and set aside.

2. Meanwhile, bring a large saucepan of lightly salted water to the boil. Add the pasta, return to the boil and cook for 8–10 minutes, or until tender but still firm to the bite. Add the beans 5 minutes before the end of the cooking time.

3. Drain the pasta and beans, shaking off the excess water, and immediately tip into a large bowl. Add the pesto and stir until the pasta and beans are well coated. Set aside to cool.

HERO TIPS

This is a perfect salad for a summer gathering. Try adding sun-blush tomatoes for a sweeter taste, or drizzle with balsamic vinegar to sharpen the flavours.

4. When the chicken is cool enough to handle, remove the skin and bones and cut the flesh into bite-sized pieces. Stir into the pesto mixture and season to taste with salt and pepper. Set aside to cool completely, then cover and chill until required. (It will keep for up to 1 day, covered, in the refrigerator.)

5. Remove the salad from the refrigerator 10 minutes before serving. Arrange the tomato slices on a serving platter. Stir the salad and add extra pesto, if needed. Mound the salad on top of the tomatoes, garnish with basil leaves and serve immediately.

CREAM OF CHICKEN SOUP

SERVES: 4

PREP TIME: 15 MINS PLUS COOLING

COOK TIME: 40 MINS

INGREDIENTS

3 tbsp butter

4 shallots, chopped

1 leek, sliced

450 g/1 lb skinless chicken breasts, chopped

600 ml/1 pint chicken stock

1 tbsp chopped fresh parsley

1 tbsp chopped fresh thyme, plus extra sprigs to garnish

175 ml/6 fl oz double cream

salt and pepper

1. Melt the butter in a large saucepan over a medium heat. Add the shallots and cook, stirring, for 3 minutes, until slightly softened.

2. Add the leek and cook for a further 5 minutes, stirring.

3. Add the chicken, stock and herbs, and season to taste with salt and pepper. Bring to the boil, then reduce the heat and simmer for 25 minutes, until the chicken is tender and cooked through. To check the chicken pieces are cooked through, cut into the middle to check that there are no remaining traces of pink or red.

4. Remove from the heat and leave to cool for 10 minutes. Transfer the soup to a food processor or blender and process until smooth (you may need to do this in batches).

5. Return the soup to the rinsed-out pan and warm over a low heat for 5 minutes.

6. Stir in the cream and cook for a further 2 minutes, then remove from the heat and ladle into warmed serving bowls. Garnish with thyme sprigs and serve immediately.

SPICY CHICKEN NOODLE SOUP

This quick, healthy, wholesome soup is a real winner for an instant meal that's packed with goodness. The main flavour comes from miso, a highly nutritious fermented paste used as the basis of many noodle soups.

SERVES: 2   **PREP TIME: 15 MINS**   **COOK TIME: 5–10 MINS**

INGREDIENTS

300 ml/10 fl oz chicken stock

250 ml/9 fl oz boiling water

1 x 18-g sachet miso paste

2-cm/¾-inch piece fresh ginger, peeled and finely grated

1 red chilli, deseeded and thinly sliced

1 carrot, peeled and cut into thin strips

200 g/7 oz pak choi, roughly chopped

150 g/5½ oz dried egg thread noodles, cooked

1 cooked chicken breast, shredded

dark soy sauce, to taste

4 spring onions, trimmed and finely chopped

handful fresh coriander, roughly chopped, to serve

1. Place the stock and boiling water in a saucepan and bring to the boil over a medium–high heat. Add the miso paste and simmer for 1–2 minutes.

2. Add the ginger, chilli, carrot, pak choi, cooked noodles and chicken. Simmer for a further 4–5 minutes. Season to taste with soy sauce.

3. Scatter the spring onions in the base of two warmed serving bowls and pour the soup over. Top with chopped coriander and serve immediately.

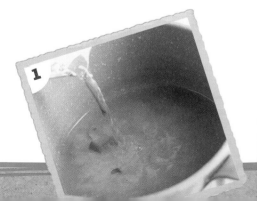

TAKE STOCK!

A good home-made stock will make a real difference to the overall flavour of many dishes, including soups, sauces, casseroles and stews, so it is well worth the effort to make your own. Home-made stock also freezes well, so it's a good idea to make a large batch and then cool and freeze it for future use.

CHICKEN STOCK

You can make two types of chicken stock: a light stock made from raw carcasses, and a brown stock made from a cooked carcass. It is more usual to prepare the latter (see recipe below) because we often have a carcass leftover from a roast chicken, whilst it is less usual to have a whole fresh carcass.

Makes about 1 litre/1¾ pints

1 carcass from a roast chicken
1.4 litres/2½ pints water
1 onion, peeled and sliced
1 carrot, peeled and sliced
1 celery stick, sliced
1 tsp dried thyme
1 bay leaf
3 sprigs fresh parsley
salt and pepper

1. Break up the chicken carcass and place it in a large (lidded) saucepan (about 3.5 litres/6 pints capacity). Add the water, vegetables and herbs. Season well and bring to the boil over a medium heat. Skim the surface if any foam forms.

2. Cover the pan with the lid, lower the heat and simmer for 1½–2 hours.

3. Remove from the heat, allow to cool a little, then strain through a sieve into a large bowl. Discard the contents of the sieve (including all the bones and any bits of meat, the vegetables and herbs).

4. Cool completely, then remove all traces of fat from the top of the stock using a slotted spoon. If required, you can then boil the stock (uncovered) for up to 30 minutes to reduce the stock and give a more intense flavour. Cover the cool stock with clingfilm, store in the refrigerator and use within 1–2 days.

Hero Tips

This stock is suitable for freezing. Chill thoroughly, then pour into a rigid, airtight (lidded) container, and freeze for up to 3 months. To use, thaw at room temperature or in the refrigerator and use as instructed.

OTHER STOCK PRODUCTS

If you are not able to make your own chicken stock, there is a good range of chicken stock products available to buy. These include stock cubes, stock granules, bouillon powder, concentrated liquid stock, chilled fresh stock, stock pots, melts or shots, as well as some reduced-salt versions.

CHICKEN, MUSHROOM & HERB OMELETTE

Part of the versatility of chicken is that any leftovers are just as good as when cooked fresh. Omelettes are the ultimate fast food. If making more than one, make them one after another and keep warm in an oven preheated to 150°C/300°F/Gas Mark 2 until they are all ready to serve.

MAKES: 1   **PREP TIME: 10–15 MINS**   **COOK TIME: 12 MINS**

INGREDIENTS

15 g/½ oz butter

2 tbsp sunflower oil

100 g/3½ oz chestnut mushrooms, trimmed and thinly sliced

55 g/2 oz cooked boneless, skinless chicken, thinly sliced

1 tbsp chopped mixed fresh herbs, such as chervil, chives, parsley and thyme, plus extra parsley to garnish

2 eggs

1 tbsp milk or water

salt and pepper

1. Melt the butter with half the oil in a 20-cm/8-inch frying pan over a medium–high heat. Add the mushrooms, season to taste with salt and pepper and fry, stirring, for 5–8 minutes until the mushrooms re-absorb the liquid they give off.

2. Add the chicken and herbs and continue frying to heat the chicken. Adjust the seasoning, if necessary. Remove from the pan and keep hot.

3. Add the remaining oil to the pan, heat until hot and swirl around the base and side. Beat the eggs with the milk and season to taste with salt and pepper.

4. When the oil is hot, pour the eggs into the pan, tilting and rotating the pan so they cover the base evenly. Reduce the heat to low–medium.

5. Cook for 5–10 seconds, or until the omelette is set on the base. Spoon the chicken mixture into the centre, then use a palette knife to ease half the omelette over the filling. Slide the omelette out of the pan, garnish with parsley and serve immediately.

SMOKED CHICKEN & HAM FOCACCIA

SERVES: 2–4   **PREP TIME: 15 MINS**   **COOK TIME: 5 MINS**

INGREDIENTS

1 thick focaccia loaf

handful of fresh basil leaves

2 small courgettes, coarsely grated

6 wafer-thin slices of smoked chicken

6 wafer-thin slices of cooked ham

225 g/8 oz taleggio cheese, cut into strips

freshly grated nutmeg (optional)

cherry tomatoes and salad leaves, to serve

1. Preheat a griddle plate or pan under the grill until both grill and griddle are hot. If you do not have a griddle, heat a heavy baking sheet instead. Slice the focaccia in half horizontally and cut the top half lengthways into strips.

2. Cover the bottom half of the focaccia with basil leaves, top with the courgettes in an even layer and cover with the chicken and ham. Lay the strips of focaccia on top, placing strips of cheese between them. Sprinkle with a little nutmeg, if using.

3. Place the assembled bread on the hot griddle and cook under the preheated grill, well away from the heat, for about 5 minutes, until the cheese has melted and the top of the bread is browned. Cut the focaccia into four pieces and serve immediately with cherry tomatoes and salad leaves.

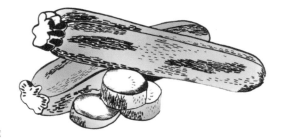

CHICKEN & LIME TACOS

MAKES: 12

PREP TIME: 15 MINS PLUS MARINATING

COOK TIME: 20 MINS

INGREDIENTS

4 boneless, skinless chicken thighs, about 300 g/10½ oz total weight

2 tbsp freshly squeezed lime juice

1 tbsp sunflower oil, plus extra for oiling

1 tsp ancho chilli powder or paprika, or to taste

1 tsp ground cumin

1 tsp ground coriander

salt and pepper

CORIANDER & LIME RICE

175 g/6 oz easy-cook long-grain rice

finely grated rind of 1 lime

2 tbsp finely chopped coriander

TO SERVE

12 crisp corn taco shells, warmed according to the packet instructions

shredded cos lettuce

guacamole

tomato salsa

mature Cheddar cheese or Red Leicester cheese, finely grated

1. Put the chicken thighs into a non-metallic dish and rub all over with the lime juice. Mix together the oil, chilli powder, cumin and ground coriander and season to taste with salt and pepper. Rub all over the chicken thighs, then set them aside to marinate for 2 hours.

2. Meanwhile, cook the rice according to the packet instructions. Drain well and transfer to a bowl. Stir in the lime rind, cover and keep warm while you cook the chicken.

3. Heat a ridged, cast-iron griddle pan over a very high heat. Brush the ridges with oil and reduce the heat to medium. Add the chicken thighs and fry for 4 minutes, brushing once with any leftover marinade. Turn and fry for a further 4 minutes, or until the chicken is cooked through and the juices run clear when a skewer is inserted into the thickest part of the meat. Slice into strips.

4. Stir the coriander into the rice and adjust the seasoning, if necessary.

5. To assemble, divide the rice between the taco shells, then add the chicken. Top with lettuce, then add any of the suggested serving accompaniments. Serve immediately.

CHICKEN BURRITO BOWLS

SERVES: 4 **PREP TIME: 10 MINS** **COOK TIME: 1¼ HRS**

INGREDIENTS

6 skinless chicken thighs on the bone, about 800 g/1 lb 12 oz total weight

1 litre/1¾ pints water

400 g/14 oz canned chopped tomatoes

2 bay leaves

2 pickled Serrano or jalapeño chillies, chopped

2 limes, sliced

1 onion, halved

1 tbsp Mexican oregano

2 tsp ancho chilli powder

2 tsp ground coriander

2 tsp ground cumin

300 g/10½ oz easy-cook long-grain rice

salt and pepper

TO SERVE

chopped fresh coriander

2 avocados, peeled, stoned, diced and tossed with lime juice

other accompaniments of your choice, such as grated cheeses, pitted black olives, soured cream and chopped jalapeño peppers

1. Put the chicken and water into a saucepan and slowly bring to the boil, skimming the surface as necessary. When the foam stops rising, stir in the tomatoes, bay leaves, chillies, lime slices, onion, oregano, chilli powder, ground coriander and cumin and season to taste with salt and pepper. Adjust the heat so the liquid just bubbles, then leave to bubble for about 60 minutes until the liquid evaporates and the meat is very tender. The juices should run clear when a skewer is inserted into the thickest part of the meat.

2. Meanwhile, cook the rice according to the packet instructions, then drain well and keep hot.

3. Use a slotted spoon to transfer the chicken to a bowl. Remove the bones and use 2 forks to shred the meat. Adjust the seasoning, if necessary.

4. To serve, divide the rice between four warmed bowls, then top with the shredded chicken. Sprinkle with chopped coriander and serve with the remaining accompaniments in small bowls for adding at the table.

CHICKEN FAJITAS

SERVES: 4

PREP TIME: 15 MINS PLUS MARINATING

COOK TIME: 12–15 MINS

INGREDIENTS

3 tbsp olive oil, plus extra for drizzling

3 tbsp maple syrup or clear honey

1 tbsp red wine vinegar

2 garlic cloves, crushed

2 tsp dried oregano

1–2 tsp dried chilli flakes

4 skinless, boneless chicken breasts

2 red peppers, deseeded and cut into 2.5-cm/1-inch strips

salt and pepper

warmed flour tortillas and shredded lettuce, to serve

1. Place the oil, maple syrup, vinegar, garlic, oregano, chilli flakes, and salt and pepper to taste in a large, shallow dish and mix together.

2. Slice the chicken across the grain into slices 2.5 cm/1 inch thick. Toss in the marinade to coat. Cover and chill for 2–3 hours, turning occasionally.

3. Drain the chicken. Heat a griddle pan until hot. Add the chicken and cook over a medium–high heat for 3–4 minutes on each side. To check that the meat is cooked through, cut into the middle to check that there are no remaining traces of pink or red. Transfer to a warmed plate.

4. Add the peppers, skin side down, to the pan and cook for 2 minutes on each side until cooked through. Transfer to the plate with the chicken.

5. Divide the chicken and peppers between the flour tortillas, top with a little shredded lettuce, wrap and serve immediately.

CAJUN CHICKEN

SERVES: 2   **PREP TIME: 10 MINS**   **COOK TIME: 25–30 MINS**

INGREDIENTS

4 chicken drumsticks

4 chicken thighs

2 fresh sweetcorn cobs, husks and silks removed

85 g/3 oz butter, melted

oil, for cooking

SPICE MIX

2 tsp onion powder

2 tsp paprika

1½ tsp salt

1 tsp garlic powder

1 tsp dried thyme

1 tsp cayenne pepper

1 tsp ground black pepper

½ tsp ground white pepper

¼ tsp ground cumin

1. Using a sharp knife, make two to three diagonal slashes in the chicken drumsticks and thighs, then place them in a large dish. Add the corn cobs. Mix all the ingredients for the spice mix together in a small bowl.

2. Brush the chicken and corn with the melted butter and sprinkle with the spice mix. Toss to coat well.

3. Heat the oil in a large griddle pan over a medium–high heat and cook the chicken, turning occasionally, for 15 minutes, then add the corn cobs and cook, turning occasionally, for a further 10–15 minutes, or until beginning to blacken slightly at the edges. Check the chicken is tender and the juices run clear when a skewer is inserted into the thickest part of the meat. Transfer to a serving plate and serve.

HERO TIPS

This summery dish is also delicious made on the barbecue. Simply place onto a preheated and lightly oiled barbecue rack and cook as instructed above.

CHICKEN & CASHEW NUTS

SERVES: 6

**PREP TIME: 20 MINS
PLUS MARINATING
AND SOAKING**

COOK TIME: 10–15 MINS

INGREDIENTS

450 g/1 lb chicken breast

3 dried Chinese mushrooms,
soaked in warm water for
20 minutes

2 tbsp vegetable oil or
groundnut oil

4 slices fresh ginger

1 tsp finely chopped garlic

1 red pepper, deseeded and cut
into 2.5-cm/1-inch squares

1 tbsp light soy sauce

85 g/3 oz cashew nuts, toasted

MARINADE

2 tbsp light soy sauce

1 tsp Shaoxing rice wine

pinch of sugar

1. Cut the chicken into cubes and put in a dish. Combine the marinade ingredients and pour over the chicken. Leave to marinate for at least 20 minutes.

2. Squeeze any excess water from the mushrooms and finely slice, discarding any tough stems. Reserve the soaking water.

3. Heat a wok over a high heat, then add 1 tablespoon of oil. Add the ginger and stir-fry until fragrant. Stir in the chicken and cook for 2 minutes, until it turns golden brown. Before the chicken is cooked through, remove and set aside.

4. Wipe out the wok with kitchen paper. Heat the wok over a high heat and add the remaining oil. Add the garlic and cook, stirring, for 1 minute. Add the mushrooms and red pepper and stir-fry for a further 2 minutes. Add about 2 tablespoons of the mushroom soaking water and cook for about 2 minutes, or until the water has evaporated.

5. Return the chicken to the wok, add the soy sauce and the cashew nuts and stir-fry for 2 minutes. Cut into the middle of the chicken to check there are no remaining traces of pink or red. Serve immediately.

JERK CHICKEN BURGERS

MAKES: 4   **PREP TIME: 25 MINS**   **COOK TIME: 20–25 MINS**

INGREDIENTS

1 tsp soft light brown sugar
1 tsp ground ginger
½ tsp ground allspice
½ tsp dried thyme
½–1 tsp cayenne pepper or chopped fresh jalapeño chilli
1 tbsp lime juice
2 garlic cloves, finely chopped
½ tsp salt
½ tsp pepper
450 g/1 lb fresh chicken mince
1 tbsp vegetable oil
1 red pepper or yellow pepper, deseeded and cut into large flat pieces
1 tsp olive oil
1 tsp red wine vinegar
4 onion rolls, split
lettuce leaves
salt and pepper

1. Place the sugar, ginger, allspice, thyme, cayenne pepper, lime juice, garlic, the salt and pepper into a bowl and mix together. Add the chicken and gently mix to combine. Divide the mixture into four equal-sized portions and shape each portion into a patty.

2. Place a griddle pan over a medium-high heat and add the vegetable oil. Add the red pepper and cook for about 5 minutes, turning frequently, until blackened. Transfer to a bowl, cover with clingfilm or a plate and leave to steam for 5 minutes. Remove the skin and cut the flesh into strips. Toss with the olive oil, vinegar, and salt and pepper to taste.

3. Put the patties in the pan and cook, covered, for about 5 minutes on each side until brown and cooked through. Place the burgers in the rolls and top with the lettuce and peppers. Serve immediately.

HERO TIPS

To spice up these burgers even more, serve with whole pickled jalapeños on the side, or use them chopped to top your burger.

PESTO CHICKEN PIZZA

Leftover chicken and pre-made pizza bases make for the perfect quick and easy supper. You can vary the toppings according to taste but this recipe is always a winner.

MAKES: 2 X 26–CM/ 10½–INCH PIZZAS   **PREP TIME: 10 MINS**   **COOK TIME: 10–12 MINS**

INGREDIENTS

2 x 26-cm/10½-inch ready-made pizza bases

8 tbsp ready-made pesto

175 g/6 oz cooked chicken, torn into strips

100 g/3½ oz canned sweetcorn, drained

6 cherry tomatoes, thinly sliced

250 g/9 oz mozzarella cheese, drained and roughly torn

salt and pepper

1. Preheat the oven to 220°C/425°F/Gas Mark 7. Place the pizza bases on two baking trays.

2. Divide the pesto between the two pizza bases, spreading almost to the edges. Scatter over the chicken, sweetcorn and tomatoes. Top with the cheese and season to taste with salt and pepper.

3. Bake in the preheated oven for 10-12 minutes, or until the cheese is melting and turning golden and the bases are crisp underneath. Serve immediately.

CHICKEN DINNERS

ROAST CHICKEN

SERVES: 6 **PREP TIME: 15 MINS** **COOK TIME: 2 HRS 10 MINS PLUS RESTING**

INGREDIENTS

1 chicken, weighing 2.25 kg/5 lb

55 g/2 oz butter, softened

2 tbsp chopped fresh lemon thyme, plus extra sprigs to garnish

1 lemon, cut into quarters

125 ml/4 fl oz white wine, plus extra if needed

salt and pepper

1. Preheat the oven to 220°C/425°F/Gas Mark 7. Place the chicken in a roasting tin. Put the butter in a bowl, then mix in the thyme, and salt and pepper to taste and use to butter the chicken.

2. Place the lemon inside the cavity. Pour the wine over and roast in the preheated oven for 15 minutes.

3. Reduce the temperature to 190°C/375°F/ Gas Mark 5 and roast, basting frequently, for a further 1¾ hours.

4. To check a whole bird is cooked through, pierce the thickest part of the leg between the drumstick and the thigh with a thin skewer. Any juices should be piping hot and clear with no traces of red or pink. To further check, gently pull the leg away from the body, the leg should 'give' and no traces of pinkness or blood should remain. Transfer to a warmed platter, cover with foil and allow to rest for 10 minutes.

5. Place the roasting tin on the hob and simmer the pan juices gently over a low heat until they have reduced and are thick and glossy. Season and reserve.

6. To carve the chicken, place on a clean chopping board. Using a carving knife and fork, cut between the wings and the side of the breast. Remove the wings and cut slices off the breast.

7. Cut the legs from the body and cut through the joint to make drumsticks and thigh portions. Serve with the pan juices, garnished with thyme sprigs.

FRIED CHICKEN WITH TOMATO & BACON SAUCE

This wonderfully rich dish can be served with so many different sides. Try it with pasta or vegetables or even just some fresh bread to help mop up all of the delicious sauce.

SERVES: 4   **PREP TIME: 20 MINS**   **COOK TIME: 45 MINS**

INGREDIENTS

25 g/1 oz butter

2 tbsp olive oil

4 skinless, boneless chicken breasts or 8 skinless, boneless chicken thighs

TOMATO & BACON SAUCE

25 g/1 oz butter

2 tbsp olive oil

1 large onion, finely chopped

2 garlic cloves, finely chopped

1 celery stick, finely chopped

4 rashers bacon, diced

400 g/14 oz canned chopped tomatoes

2 tbsp tomato purée

brown sugar, to taste

100 ml/3½ fl oz water

1 tbsp chopped fresh basil

1 tbsp chopped fresh flat-leaf parsley, plus extra to garnish

salt and pepper

1. First, make the tomato and bacon sauce. Melt the butter with the oil in a large saucepan. Add the onion, garlic, celery and bacon and cook over a low heat, stirring occasionally, for 5 minutes, until softened. Stir in the tomatoes, tomato purée, sugar to taste and water and season to taste with salt and pepper. Increase the heat to medium and bring to the boil, then reduce the heat and simmer, stirring occasionally, for 15–20 minutes, until thickened.

2. Meanwhile, melt the butter with the oil in a large frying pan. Add the chicken and cook over a medium–high heat for 4–5 minutes on each side, until evenly browned.

3. Stir the basil and parsley into the sauce. Add the chicken and spoon the sauce over it. Cover and simmer for 10–15 minutes. Check the chicken is cooked through and the juices run clear when a skewer is inserted into the thickest part of the meat. Garnish with parsley and serve.

MOZZARELLA-STUFFED CHICKEN BREASTS

SERVES: 4　　　**PREP TIME: 15 MINS**　　　**COOK TIME: 15–20 MINS**

INGREDIENTS

4 skinless chicken breast fillets
4 tsp ready-made pesto
125 g/4½ oz mozzarella cheese
4 thin slices Parma ham
250 g/9 oz cherry plum tomatoes, halved
75 ml/2½ fl oz dry white wine or chicken stock
1 tbsp olive oil
salt and pepper
fresh ciabatta, to serve

1. Preheat the oven to 220°C/425°F/Gas Mark 7. Place the chicken breasts on a board and cut a deep pocket into each with a sharp knife.

2. Place a teaspoonful of pesto in each pocket.

3. Cut the cheese into four equal pieces and divide between the chicken breasts, tucking into the pockets.

4. Wrap a slice of ham around each chicken breast to enclose the filling, with the join underneath.

5. Place the chicken in a shallow ovenproof dish and arrange the tomatoes around it.

6. Season with salt and pepper, pour over the wine and drizzle with the oil.

7. Bake in the preheated oven for 15–20 minutes, or until cooked through and the juices run clear when a skewer is inserted into the thickest part of the meat.

8. Cut the chicken breasts in half diagonally, place on serving plates with the tomatoes and spoon over the juices. Serve the chicken with chunks of ciabatta.

CHICKEN WITH CHILLI & CORIANDER BUTTER

SERVES: 4   **PREP TIME: 15 MINS**   **COOK TIME: 20 MINS**

INGREDIENTS

55 g/2 oz butter, softened

1 fresh bird's eye chilli, deseeded and chopped

3 tbsp chopped fresh coriander

4 skinless, boneless chicken breasts, about 175 g/6 oz each

400 ml/14 fl oz coconut milk

350 ml/12 fl oz chicken stock

200 g/7 oz basmati rice

salt and pepper

PICKLED VEGETABLES

1 carrot

½ cucumber

3 spring onions

2 tbsp rice vinegar

1. Mix the butter with the chilli and coriander.

2. Cut a deep slash into the side of each chicken breast to form a pocket.

3. Spoon a quarter of the butter into each pocket and place on a 30-cm/12-inch square of baking paper.

4. Season to taste with salt and pepper, then bring two opposite sides of the paper together on top, folding over to seal firmly. Twist the ends to seal.

5. Pour the coconut milk and stock into a large saucepan with a steamer top. Bring to the boil. Stir in the rice with a pinch of salt.

6. Place the chicken parcels in the steamer top, cover and simmer for 15–18 minutes, stirring the rice once, until the rice is tender and the chicken juices run clear when a skewer is inserted into the thickest part of the meat.

7. Meanwhile, trim the carrot, cucumber and spring onions and cut into fine matchsticks. Sprinkle with the rice vinegar.

8. Unwrap the chicken, reserving the juices, and cut in half diagonally. Serve the chicken over the rice, with the juices spooned over and pickled vegetables on the side.

YAKI SOBA

SERVES: 2   **PREP TIME: 15 MINS**   **COOK TIME: APPROX. 10 MINS**

INGREDIENTS

400 g/14 oz ramen noodles
1 onion, finely sliced
200 g/7 oz beansprouts
1 red pepper, deseeded and sliced
150 g/5½ oz chicken, cooked and sliced
12 cooked peeled prawns
1 tbsp oil, for stir-frying
2 tbsp shoyu
½ tbsp mirin
1 tsp sesame oil
1 tsp sesame seeds
2 spring onions, finely sliced

1. Cook the noodles according to the packet instructions, drain well, and tip into a bowl.

2. Mix together the onion, beansprouts, red pepper, chicken and prawns in a bowl. Stir through the noodles. Meanwhile, preheat a wok over a high heat, add the oil and heat until very hot.

3. Add the noodle mixture and stir-fry for 4 minutes, or until golden, then add the shoyu, mirin and sesame oil and toss together.

4. Divide the noodles between two bowls.

5. Sprinkle with sesame seeds and spring onions and serve.

HERO TIPS

If you are in a hurry you can buy yaki soba kits from Asian supermarkets or online stores. To speed things up even more – and for any vegetarian guests – this recipe works equally well made with fresh vegetables and omitting the meat.

GREEN CHICKEN CURRY

This curry would be delicious with straight-to-wok noodles. Stir them into the curry when the chicken is cooked.

SERVES: 4   **PREP TIME: 10 MINS**   **COOK TIME: 15 MINS**

INGREDIENTS

2 tbsp groundnut or vegetable oil

4 spring onions, roughly chopped

2 tbsp green curry paste

700 ml/1¼ pints canned coconut milk

1 chicken stock cube

6 skinless chicken breasts, cut into 2.5-cm/1-inch cubes

large handful of fresh coriander, chopped

½ tsp salt

cooked rice, to serve

1. Heat a wok over a medium–high heat, then add the oil. Add the spring onions and stir-fry for 30 seconds, or until starting to soften.

2. Add the curry paste, coconut milk and stock cube and bring gently to the boil, stirring occasionally.

3. Add the chicken, half the coriander and the salt and stir well. Reduce the heat and simmer gently for 8–10 minutes, or until the chicken is cooked through. To check the chicken pieces are cooked through, cut into the middle to check that there are no remaining traces of pink or red. Stir in the remaining coriander. Serve immediately with freshly cooked rice.

CHICKEN FEED!

• Most whole fresh chickens sold in supermarkets and butchers are oven-ready and are often trussed (tied with string). Check the 'use-by' date on the label and choose a plump bird (or chicken portions) with whitish pink or golden yellow skin (depending on the variety – corn-fed chickens will have a golden yellow hue to their skin and flesh, for example) with no dry patches or signs of damage or blemishes. Larger birds tend to be better value as they have a larger proportion of meat to bone.

• Store fresh chicken loosely covered (with clingfilm or foil) in a shallow dish or container in the refrigerator for up to 2 days (or according to the 'use-by' date on the label). If you buy a whole chicken that has come with giblets, remove the giblets and keep them in a separate covered container in the refrigerator and use within 1 day (or discard the giblets if you are not going to be using them). Chicken livers and minced chicken should ideally be used within 24 hours of purchase.

• Store raw chicken on a low shelf in the coldest part of your refrigerator to prevent any juices dripping or leaking onto any foods below and to avoid the risk of cross-contamination. Remember that raw and cooked chicken should always be stored separately.

• Freeze chicken on the day of purchase. Fresh raw chicken can be frozen for up to 3 months (and cooked chicken can be frozen for up to 2 months). Frozen chicken should be thawed in the refrigerator overnight (in a dish to catch any dripping juices) until it is completely thawed. It should then be cooked as soon as possible and within 24 hours. Do not re-freeze thawed chicken, however, you can freeze it again once it is cooked.

• It is essential to store, handle and cook chicken correctly as raw or undercooked chicken may contain harmful bacteria, such as salmonella, that can cause food poisoning. Always wash your hands thoroughly before and after handling raw or cooked chicken, and make sure work surfaces and utensils are cleaned with hot soapy water. Disinfect worktops after use, preferably with a mild detergent or an antibacterial cleaner, and always use separate chopping boards and utensils when preparing raw and cooked chicken.

• Always make sure the chicken is thoroughly cooked before serving – it should be piping hot throughout and there should be no signs of pinkness when you cut into the thickest part of the meat. If you are roasting a whole bird, it is cooked when you pierce the thickest part of the thigh with a fork or skewer and the juices run clear. If the juices are pink or there are traces of blood, continue roasting the chicken until the juices run clear.

• Store leftover cooked chicken in a covered or airtight container in the refrigerator and use within 1–2 days. If you are reheating dishes containing chicken, make sure they are reheated thoroughly and are piping hot throughout before serving.

INDIVIDUAL CHICKEN PIES

MAKES: 6   **PREP TIME: 25 MINS**   **COOK TIME: 1 HR 20 MINS PLUS STANDING**

INGREDIENTS

1 tbsp olive oil

225 g/8 oz button mushrooms, sliced

1 onion, finely chopped

350 g/12 oz carrots, sliced

2 celery sticks, sliced

1 litre/1¾ pints cold chicken stock

85 g/3 oz butter

55 g/2 oz plain flour, plus extra for dusting

900 g/2 lb skinless, boneless chicken breasts, cut into 2.5-cm/1-inch cubes

115 g/4 oz frozen peas

1 tsp chopped fresh thyme

675 g/1 lb 8 oz ready-made shortcrust pastry

1 egg, lightly beaten

salt and pepper

1. Preheat the oven to 200°C/400°F/Gas Mark 6. Heat the oil in a large saucepan. Add the mushrooms and onion and cook over a medium heat, stirring frequently, for 8 minutes until golden.

2. Add the carrots, celery and half the stock and bring to the boil. Reduce the heat to low and simmer for 12–15 minutes until the vegetables are almost tender.

3. Meanwhile, melt the butter in a large saucepan over a medium heat. Whisk in the flour and cook, stirring constantly, for 4 minutes.

4. Gradually whisk in the remaining stock, then reduce the heat to low–medium and simmer, stirring, until thick. Stir in the vegetable mixture and add the chicken, peas and thyme.

5. Simmer, stirring constantly, for 5 minutes. Taste and adjust the seasoning, adding salt and pepper if needed. Divide the mixture between six large ramekins.

6. Roll out the pastry on a floured surface and cut out six rounds, each 2.5 cm/1 inch larger than the diameter of the ramekins.

7. Place the pastry rounds on top of the filling, then crimp the edges. Cut a small cross in the centre of each round.

8. Put the ramekins on a baking sheet and brush the tops with beaten egg. Bake in the preheated oven for 35–40 minutes, until golden brown and bubbling. Leave to stand for 15 minutes before serving.

CHICKEN TRAY BAKE

Like most casserole-style dishes this recipe is equally good served the day it is cooked or up to a day later. If you are reheating, bring the vegetables to the boil, then return the chicken pieces to the pan and reduce the heat to avoid over-cooking the chicken.

SERVES: 4　　　　**PREP TIME: 10 MINS**　　　　**COOK TIME: 50 MINS**

INGREDIENTS

4 chicken legs, about 350 g/12 oz each
2 tbsp olive oil
2 red peppers, deseeded and thickly sliced
1 large courgette, halved lengthways and thinly sliced
1 large onion, finely chopped
1 fennel bulb, thickly sliced lengthways
800 g/1 lb 12 oz canned chopped tomatoes
1 tbsp dried dill
1 tbsp balsamic vinegar
pinch of soft light brown sugar
salt and pepper
fresh crusty bread, to serve

1. Preheat the oven to 190°C/375°F/Gas Mark 5. Leave the chicken legs whole or cut them into drumsticks and thighs.

2. Heat the oil in a frying pan. Add the chicken pieces, working in batches, if necessary, and fry for 5–7 minutes until golden brown. Remove from the pan and keep hot.

3. Pour off all but 2 tablespoons of the oil. Add the red peppers, courgette, onion and fennel and fry, stirring, for 3–5 minutes until the onion is soft. Stir in the tomatoes, dill, vinegar and sugar and season with salt and pepper.

4. Bring to the boil, stirring. Place the chicken pieces on a baking sheet and pour the vegetables over. Cover tightly with foil, shiny side down.

5. Bake in the preheated oven for 30–35 minutes until the chicken is cooked through and the juices run clear when a skewer is inserted into the thickest part of the meat. Serve with crusty bread.

CHEDDAR & APPLE-STUFFED CHICKEN BREASTS

SERVES: 4   **PREP TIME: 15 MINS**   **COOK TIME: 25–30 MINS PLUS STANDING**

INGREDIENTS

4 thick boneless, skinless chicken breasts, about 200 g/7 oz each

1 tbsp sunflower oil, plus extra for oiling

1 small onion, finely chopped

1 celery stick, finely chopped

¼ tsp dried sage

1 eating apple, about 150 g/5½ oz, cored and diced

85 g/3 oz mature Cheddar cheese, coarsely grated

2 tbsp finely chopped parsley, plus extra to garnish

6 slices Parma ham

salt and pepper

cooked green vegetables, to serve

1. Preheat the oven to 190°C/375°F/Gas Mark 5 and lightly oil a small roasting tin.

2. Put a chicken breast on a chopping board, rounded side up. Use a small, sharp knife to cut a pocket along the length of the breast, cutting as deep as you can without cutting through to the other side or the ends. Repeat with the remaining chicken breasts, then set aside.

3. To make the stuffing, heat the oil in a frying pan, add the onion, celery and sage and fry, stirring, for 3–5 minutes until soft. Stir in the apple and fry for a further 2 minutes until it is soft but not falling apart. Stir in the cheese and parsley and season with salt and pepper.

4. Divide the stuffing between the breast pockets. Wrap 1½ slices of ham around each breast, then rub the tops with a little oil.

5. Transfer to the prepared tin and roast in the preheated oven for 20–25 minutes, or until the chicken is cooked through and the juices run clear when a skewer is inserted into the thickest part of the meat. Remove from the oven, cover with foil and leave to stand for 3–5 minutes before serving with green vegetables.

SPICED CHICKEN STEW

SERVES: 6

PREP TIME: 10 MINS

**COOK TIME:
APPROX. 1½ HRS**

INGREDIENTS

1.8 kg/4 lb chicken pieces

2 tbsp paprika

2 tbsp olive oil

25 g/1 oz butter

450 g/1 lb onions, chopped

2 yellow peppers, deseeded
and chopped

400 g/14 oz canned chopped
tomatoes

225 ml/8 fl oz dry white wine

450 ml/16 fl oz chicken stock

1 tbsp Worcestershire sauce

½ tsp Tabasco sauce

1 tbsp finely chopped fresh
flat-leaf parsley, plus extra
to garnish

325 g/11½ oz canned
sweetcorn kernels, drained

425 g/15 oz canned butter
beans, drained and rinsed

2 tbsp plain flour

4 tbsp water

salt

1. Season the chicken pieces well with salt and dust with the paprika.

2. Heat the oil and butter in a flameproof casserole or large saucepan. Add the chicken pieces and cook over a medium heat, turning, for 10–15 minutes, or until browned all over. Transfer to a plate with a slotted spoon.

3. Add the onions and peppers to the casserole. Cook over a low heat, stirring occasionally, for 5 minutes, or until softened. Add the tomatoes, wine, stock, Worcestershire sauce, Tabasco sauce and parsley and bring to the boil, stirring. Return the chicken to the casserole, cover and simmer, stirring occasionally, for 30 minutes.

4. Add the sweetcorn and butter beans to the casserole, partially re-cover and simmer for a further 30 minutes, or until the chicken is tender and the juices run clear when a skewer is inserted into the thickest part of the meat. Place the flour and water in a small bowl and mix to make a paste. Stir a ladleful of the cooking liquid into the paste, then stir the paste into the stew. Cook, stirring frequently, for a further 5 minutes. Garnish with parsley and serve immediately.

CHICKEN KIEV

This well-loved chicken classic is surprisingly easy to make. The garlic-butter helps keep the chicken beautifully moist and the breadcrumbs offer a delicious golden crunch.

MAKES: 8

PREP TIME: 15 MINS PLUS CHILLING

COOK TIME: APPROX. 30 MINS

INGREDIENTS

115 g/4 oz butter, softened

3–4 garlic cloves, very finely chopped

1 tbsp chopped fresh parsley

1 tbsp snipped fresh chives

juice and finely grated rind of ½ lemon

8 skinless, boneless chicken breasts, about 115 g/4 oz each

55 g/2 oz plain flour

2 eggs, lightly beaten

175 g/6 oz dry breadcrumbs

groundnut oil or sunflower oil, for deep-frying

salt and pepper

cooked green vegetables, to serve

1. Beat the butter in a bowl with the garlic, herbs, and lemon juice and rind. Season to taste with salt and pepper. Divide into eight pieces, then shape into cylinders. Wrap in foil and chill in the refrigerator until firm.

2. Place each chicken breast between two sheets of clingfilm. Pound gently with a meat mallet or rolling pin to flatten the chicken to an even thickness. Place a butter cylinder on each chicken piece and roll up. Secure with cocktail sticks.

3. Place the flour, eggs and breadcrumbs in separate shallow dishes. Dip the rolls into the flour, then the egg and, finally, the breadcrumbs. Chill in the refrigerator for 1 hour.

4. Heat enough oil for deep-frying in a saucepan or deep-fat fryer to 180–190°C/350–375°F, or until a cube of bread browns in 30 seconds. Deep-fry the chicken, in batches, for 8–10 minutes, or until cooked through and golden brown. Drain on kitchen paper. Serve immediately with green vegetables.

CHICKEN BREASTS BRAISED WITH BABY VEGETABLES

The perfect thing about this dish is that it is all cooked in one pot, saving on both time and washing up. It serves as a great Sunday roast alternative.

SERVES: 4　　　　**PREP TIME: 10 MINS**　　　　**COOK TIME: 30 MINS**

INGREDIENTS

4 skinless chicken breasts
15 g/½ oz butter
1 tbsp olive oil
8 shallots
250 ml/9 fl oz chicken stock
12 baby carrots
8 baby turnips
2 bay leaves
140 g/5 oz fresh or frozen peas
salt and pepper
boiled new potatoes, to serve

1. Cut deep slashes through the chicken at intervals and sprinkle with salt and pepper.

2. Heat the butter and oil in a wide, flameproof casserole or saucepan, add the chicken breasts and shallots and fry, turning, for 3–4 minutes until golden brown.

3. Add the stock and bring to the boil, then add the carrots, turnips and bay leaves. Reduce the heat, cover and simmer gently for 20 minutes.

4. Stir in the peas and cook for a further 5 minutes. Check the chicken and vegetables are tender and the juices of the meat run clear when a skewer is inserted into the thickest part of the meat.

5. Remove and discard the bay leaves, adjust the seasoning to taste and serve with new potatoes.

CREAMY CHICKEN PENNE

SERVES: 2　　　　**PREP TIME: 5 MINS**　　　　**COOK TIME: APPROX. 20 MINS**

INGREDIENTS

200 g/7 oz dried penne

1 tbsp olive oil

2 skinless, boneless chicken breasts

4 tbsp dry white wine

115 g/4 oz frozen peas

5 tbsp double cream

salt

4–5 tbsp chopped fresh flat-leaf parsley, to garnish

1. Bring a large saucepan of lightly salted water to the boil. Add the pasta, bring back to the boil and cook for about 8–10 minutes, until tender but still firm to the bite.

2. Meanwhile, heat the oil in a frying pan. Add the chicken and cook over a medium heat for about 4 minutes on each side.

3. Pour in the wine and cook over a high heat until it has almost evaporated.

4. Drain the pasta. Add the peas, cream and pasta to the frying pan and stir well. Cover and simmer for 2 minutes. Check the chicken is cooked through and the juices run clear when a skewer is inserted into the thickest part of the meat.

5. Garnish the chicken and pasta mixture with parsley and serve immediately.

HERO TIPS

For a healthier version, use light soured cream instead of the double cream. Or if you want to up the calorie intake, garnish with grated Parmesan cheese!

FOOD FOR FRIENDS

CHICKEN RISOTTO WITH SAFFRON

SERVES: 4 **PREP TIME: 5 MINS** **COOK TIME: APPROX. 45 MINS**

INGREDIENTS

125 g/4½ oz butter

900 g/2 lb skinless, boneless chicken breasts, thinly sliced

1 large onion, chopped

500 g/1 lb 2 oz risotto rice

150 ml/5 fl oz white wine

1 tsp crumbled saffron threads

1.3 litres/2¼ pints hot chicken stock

55 g/2 oz Parmesan cheese, grated

salt and pepper

1. Heat 55 g/2 oz of the butter in a deep saucepan. Add the chicken and onion and cook, stirring frequently, for 8 minutes, or until golden brown and cooked through. To check the chicken pieces are cooked through, cut into the middle to check that there are no remaining traces of pink or red.

2. Add the rice and mix to coat in the butter. Cook, stirring constantly, for 2–3 minutes, or until the grains are translucent.

3. Add the wine and cook, stirring constantly, for 1 minute, until reduced.

4. Mix the saffron with 4 tablespoons of the hot stock. Add the liquid to the rice and cook, stirring constantly, until it is absorbed.

5. Gradually add the remaining hot stock, a ladleful at a time. Add more liquid as the rice absorbs each addition. Cook, stirring, for 20 minutes, or until all the liquid is absorbed and the rice is creamy.

6. Remove from the heat and add the remaining butter. Mix well, then stir in the Parmesan cheese until it melts. Season to taste with salt and pepper. Spoon the risotto into warmed serving dishes and serve immediately.

CHICKEN PARMESAN

SERVES: 4　　　　**PREP TIME: 15 MINS**　　　　**COOK TIME: APPROX. 1 HR**

INGREDIENTS

100 g/3½ oz plain flour

2 eggs

200 g/7 oz dry breadcrumbs

4 skinless, boneless chicken breasts, 250 g/9 oz each

2 tbsp olive oil, plus extra if needed

250 g/9 oz mozzarella, sliced

125 g/4½ oz Parmesan cheese, grated

salt and pepper

chopped fresh flat-leaf parsley, to garnish

SIMPLE MARINARA SAUCE

2 tbsp olive oil

1 large onion, chopped

2 large garlic cloves, chopped

1 tbsp dried mixed herbs

800 g/1 lb 12 oz canned chopped tomatoes

250 ml/9 fl oz passata

2 tsp dried oregano

pinch of sugar

1. To make the sauce, heat the oil in a large saucepan. Add the onion and fry, stirring, for 2 minutes. Add the garlic and cook, stirring, until the onion is soft. Stir in the mixed herbs, tomatoes, passata, oregano and sugar and season to taste. Bring to the boil, then cover and simmer for 15 minutes. Transfer to a blender or food processor and purée.

2. Meanwhile, preheat the oven to 200°C/400°F/ Gas Mark 6. Spread the flour over a plate. Beat the eggs in a wide bowl, and put the breadcrumbs on another plate. Halve the chicken breasts horizontally.

3. Place the chicken pieces between sheets of clingfilm and pound with a meat mallet or rolling pin until about 5 mm/¼ inch thick. Season both sides with salt and pepper. Dust a chicken breast with flour, shaking off the excess, then dip in the egg to coat. Dip in the breadcrumbs to coat both sides, then set aside and repeat with the remaining chicken pieces.

4. Heat the oil in a frying pan over a medium–high heat. Add as many chicken pieces as will fit in the pan in a single layer and fry on each side for 2 minutes, or until the chicken is golden, cooked through and the juices run clear when a skewer is inserted into the thickest part of the meat. Fry the remaining pieces, adding extra oil, if necessary. Pour half of the sauce into a baking dish that will hold the chicken in a single layer. Arrange the chicken on top, then pour over the remaining sauce. Arrange the mozzarella on top and sprinkle over the Parmesan cheese. Bake in the preheated oven for 20–25 minutes, or until the cheese is melted, golden and bubbling. Leave to stand for 5 minutes, then garnish with parsley and serve immediately.

CHICKEN & WILD MUSHROOM CANNELLONI

SERVES: 4　　　　**PREP TIME: 20 MINS**　　　　**COOK TIME: 1 HR 50 MINS**

INGREDIENTS

butter, for greasing

2 tbsp olive oil

2 garlic cloves, crushed

1 large onion, finely chopped

225 g/8 oz wild mushrooms, sliced

350 g/12 oz fresh chicken mince

115 g/4 oz prosciutto, diced

150 ml/5 fl oz Marsala wine

200 g/7 oz canned chopped tomatoes

1 tbsp shredded fresh basil leaves

2 tbsp tomato purée

10–12 dried cannelloni tubes

600 ml Béchamel sauce

85 g/3 oz freshly grated Parmesan cheese

salt and pepper

1. Preheat the oven to 190°C/375°F/Gas Mark 5. Lightly grease a large ovenproof dish. Heat the olive oil in a heavy-based frying pan. Add the garlic, onion and mushrooms and cook over a low heat, stirring frequently, for 8–10 minutes. Add the chicken mince and prosciutto and cook, stirring frequently, for 12 minutes, or until browned all over. Stir in the Marsala, tomatoes, basil and tomato purée and cook for 4 minutes. Season to taste with salt and pepper, then cover and simmer for 30 minutes. Uncover, stir and simmer for 15 minutes.

2. Meanwhile, bring a large heavy-based saucepan of lightly salted water to the boil. Add the cannelloni, bring back to the boil and cook for 8–10 minutes, or until just tender but still firm to the bite. Using a slotted spoon, transfer to a plate and pat dry.

3. Using a teaspoon, fill the cannelloni tubes with the chicken and mushroom mixture. Transfer them to the dish. Pour the Béchamel sauce over them to cover completely and sprinkle with the grated Parmesan cheese.

4. Bake in the preheated oven for 30 minutes, or until golden brown and bubbling. Serve immediately.

SPATCHCOCKED CHICKEN WITH LEMON & HONEY

SERVES: 4

PREP TIME: 10 MINS PLUS MARINATING

COOK TIME: 45–55 MINS

INGREDIENTS

2 tbsp clear honey

1 tbsp freshly squeezed lemon juice

¼ tsp hot or sweet paprika, to taste

1 chicken, about 1.5 k g/ 3 lb 5 oz, spatchcocked

sunflower oil, for oiling

salt and pepper

finely chopped fresh flat-leaf parsley and finely grated lemon rind, to garnish

1. Mix together the honey, lemon juice, paprika, and salt and pepper to taste in a wide, non-metallic bowl, large enough to hold the chicken flat.

2. Add the chicken and rub in the mixture all over, then leave to stand for 30 minutes at room temperature.

3. Meanwhile, preheat the oven to 190°C/375°F/ Gas Mark 5. Put a greased rack into a roasting tin large enough to hold the chicken flat.

4. When ready to cook, oil two long metal skewers. Place the chicken on a chopping board and run the skewers through the body in an X shape.

5. Place the chicken on the prepared rack, skin side up, and brush with the marinade. Roast in the preheated oven for 45–55 minutes, brushing with the marinade twice, until the skin is golden brown and the juices run clear when the thickest part of the meat is pierced with a skewer.

6. Remove from the oven, cover with foil and leave to rest for 5 minutes. Use a metal spoon to skim the fat off the pan juices. Carve the chicken, spoon over the pan juices and garnish with the parsley and lemon rind.

HIT THE SAUCE!

A fresh whole chicken or pieces or portions/joints of chicken can be marinated before cooking to tenderize the flesh and add flavour and moisture. Rubs can also be used to season the chicken before cooking, and many different sauces can be cooked or served with chicken to add extra flavour. The following quick and easy recipes give examples of a marinade, rub and sauce, all of which are suitable for chicken.

When roasting a whole chicken, you can also add flavour to the meat in several simple ways:

• Put a whole lemon or small orange (pierced a couple of times), a peeled onion, or a few sprigs of fresh herbs and peeled garlic cloves, inside the cavity of the bird before roasting.

• Gently insert citrus fruit slices (lemon or orange are ideal) or fresh herb sprigs (thyme, rosemary or marjoram work well) under the skin covering the breast, before roasting.

• Carefully spread a flavoured butter (such as garlic or herb butter) under the skin covering the breast, before roasting.

• Brush the outside of a whole chicken with oil, then sprinkle with ground spices or a spice seasoning mix, or dried herbs or a mixed herb seasoning of your choice, to add extra flavour and colour.

STICKY BARBECUE MARINADE

This tasty marinade cooks to a gloriously sticky, flavoursome coating and is especially good with chicken.

Makes enough for about 500 g/1 lb 2 oz prepared chicken portions

55 g/2 oz soft light or dark brown sugar
5 tbsp plum jam
2 tbsp tomato purée
2 tbsp white wine vinegar
1 tbsp wholegrain mustard

1. Heat all the ingredients together in a saucepan over a low heat, stirring until smooth. Remove from the heat and leave to cool.

2. Score the chicken portions deeply with a sharp knife. Put the prepared chicken in a shallow, non-metallic dish or polythene food bag.

3. Pour the cold marinade over the prepared chicken and turn to coat all over. Cover tightly or seal and leave to marinate in the refrigerator,

turning occasionally, for at least 1 hour or preferably overnight, before cooking.

Hero Tips

• Try using other types of preserves, such as apricot jam, redcurrant jelly or marmalade, in place of the plum jam.

• Marinade that has been used to marinate raw chicken should not be used on cooked chicken, nor should it be used to baste chicken during cooking, especially towards the end of the cooking time.

CAJUN BLACKENED SPICE RUB

Use this tasty rub to add flavour to chicken pieces before cooking.

Makes about 4 tbsp

1 tbsp cracked black peppercorns
2 tsp paprika
2 tsp garlic powder or crushed garlic
2 tsp salt
1 tsp dried thyme
1 tsp dried oregano
1 tsp mustard powder
½ tsp cayenne pepper

1. Mix all the ingredients together in a small bowl until thoroughly combined.

2. Rub the spice mixture thoroughly into the chicken, just before cooking if short of time, or preferably several hours before cooking.

3. Put the prepared chicken in a shallow dish, cover tightly, and chill in the refrigerator until you are ready to cook it.

SATAY SAUCE

Satay sauce is a tasty accompaniment or dip for grilled or barbecued chicken kebabs, chicken pieces or chicken satay skewers.

Makes about 225 ml/8 fl oz

4 spring onions, coarsely chopped
1 garlic clove, coarsely chopped
2 tsp chopped fresh ginger
6 tbsp peanut butter
1 tsp muscovado sugar
1 tsp Thai fish sauce
2 tbsp soy sauce
1 tbsp chilli sauce or Tabasco sauce
1 tsp lemon juice
salt
peanuts, to garnish

1. Put all the ingredients into a food processor. Add 150 ml/5 fl oz water and process to a purée.

2. Transfer to a saucepan, season to taste with salt and heat gently, stirring occasionally. Transfer to a bowl and sprinkle with the peanuts to garnish. Serve warm or cold.

CHICKEN BASQUAISE

SERVES: 4　　　　　**PREP TIME: 10 MINS**　　　　　**COOK TIME: 1 HR 20 MINS**

INGREDIENTS

2 tbsp plain flour

1 chicken, weighing 1.3 kg/3 lb, cut into 8 pieces

3 tbsp olive oil

1 Spanish onion, thickly sliced

2 red or yellow peppers, deseeded and cut into thick strips

2 garlic cloves

150 g/5½ oz chorizo sausage, cut into 1-cm/½-inch pieces

1 tbsp tomato purée

200 g/7 oz long-grain rice

450 ml/16 fl oz chicken stock

1 tsp chilli flakes

½ tsp dried thyme

115 g/4 oz prosciutto, diced

12 dry-cured black olives

salt and pepper

chopped fresh flat-leaf parsley, to garnish

1. Put the flour in a polythene bag and season well with salt and pepper. Add the chicken pieces to the bag, tie the top and shake well to coat. Heat 2 tablespoons of the oil in a large, flameproof casserole over a medium–high heat. Add the chicken and cook, turning frequently, for about 15 minutes, until browned all over. Transfer to a plate.

2. Heat the remaining oil in the casserole and add the onion and peppers. Reduce the heat to medium and fry until beginning to colour and soften. Add the garlic, chorizo and tomato purée and cook, stirring constantly, for about 3 minutes. Add the rice and cook, stirring to coat, for about 2 minutes, until the grains are translucent.

3. Add the stock, chilli flakes and thyme to the casserole. Season to taste with salt and pepper. Stir well and bring to the boil, then return the chicken to the casserole, pressing it gently into the rice. Cover and cook over a very low heat for about 45 minutes, until the rice is tender and the chicken juices run clear when a skewer is inserted into the thickest part of the meat.

4. Gently stir the prosciutto and olives into the rice mixture. Re-cover and heat through for a further 5 minutes. Garnish with parsley and serve immediately.

COQ AU VIN

This rich Burgundian stew was once the farmhouse cook's modest way of tenderizing and flavouring tough old birds. Today though it must be one of France's best-loved and well-known dishes.

SERVES: 4　　　　**PREP TIME: 10 MINS**　　　　**COOK TIME: APPROX. 1 HR 20 MINS**

INGREDIENTS

55 g/2 oz butter
2 tbsp olive oil
1.8 kg/4 lb chicken pieces
115 g/4 oz rindless smoked bacon, cut into strips
115 g/4 oz baby onions
115 g/4 oz chestnut mushrooms, halved
2 garlic cloves, finely chopped
2 tbsp brandy
225 ml/8 fl oz red wine
300 ml/10 fl oz chicken stock
1 bouquet garni
2 tbsp plain flour
salt and pepper
bay leaves, to garnish

1. Melt half the butter with the oil in a large flameproof casserole. Add the chicken and cook over a medium heat, stirring, for 8–10 minutes, or until browned all over. Add the bacon, onions, mushrooms and garlic.

2. Pour in the brandy and set it alight with a match or taper. When the flames have died down, add the wine, stock and bouquet garni and season to taste with salt and pepper. Bring to the boil, reduce the heat and simmer gently for 1 hour, or until the chicken is tender and the juices run clear when a skewer is inserted into the thickest part of the meat.

3. Remove and discard the bouquet garni. Transfer the chicken to a large plate and keep warm. Mix the flour with the remaining butter and whisk the beurre manié into the casserole, a little at a time. Bring to the boil, return the chicken to the casserole and heat through. Garnish with bay leaves and serve immediately (do not eat the bay leaves).

CHICKEN GUMBO

SERVES: 4–6   **PREP TIME: 30 MINS**   **COOK TIME: 2½ HRS**

INGREDIENTS

1 chicken, weighing 1.5 kg/
3 lb 5 oz, cut into 6 pieces

2 celery sticks, 1 broken in half
and 1 finely chopped

1 carrot, chopped

2 onions, 1 sliced and
1 chopped

2 bay leaves

¼ tsp salt

4 tbsp corn oil or groundnut oil

50 g/1¾ oz plain flour

2 large garlic cloves, crushed

1 green pepper, cored,
deseeded and diced

450 g/1 lb fresh okra, trimmed,
then cut crossways into
1-cm/½-inch slices

225 g/8 oz andouille sausage or
Polish kielbasa, sliced

2 tbsp tomato purée

1 tsp dried thyme

½ tsp salt

½ tsp cayenne pepper

¼ tsp pepper

400 g/14 oz canned
plum tomatoes

cooked long-grain rice and hot
pepper sauce, to serve

1. Put the chicken into a large saucepan with water to cover over a medium–high heat and bring to the boil, skimming the surface to remove the foam. When the foam stops rising, reduce the heat to medium, add the celery stick halves, carrot, sliced onion, 1 bay leaf and salt and simmer for 20 minutes, or until the chicken is tender and the juices run clear when a skewer is inserted into the thickest part of the meat. Strain the chicken, reserving 1 litre/1¾ pints of the liquid. When the chicken is cool enough to handle, remove and discard the skin, bones and flavourings. Cut the flesh into bite-sized pieces and reserve.

2. Heat the oil in a large saucepan over a medium–high heat for 2 minutes. Reduce the heat to low, sprinkle in the flour and stir to make the roux. Stir constantly for around 20 minutes, or until the roux turns hazelnut-brown. If black specks appear, it is burnt and you will have to start again.

3. Add the chopped celery, chopped onion, garlic, green pepper and okra to the saucepan. Increase the heat to medium–high and cook, stirring frequently, for 5 minutes. Add the sausage and cook, stirring frequently, for 2 minutes.

4. Stir in the remaining ingredients, including the second bay leaf and the reserved cooking liquid. Bring to the boil, crushing the tomatoes with a wooden spoon. Reduce the heat to low–medium and simmer, uncovered, for 30 minutes, stirring occasionally.

5. Add the chicken to the pan and simmer for a further 30 minutes. Taste and adjust the seasoning, if necessary. Remove and discard the bay leaves and spoon the gumbo over the rice. Serve with a bottle of hot pepper sauce on the side.

BAKED CHICKEN & CHORIZO PAELLA

SERVES: 4   **PREP TIME: 20 MINS**   **COOK TIME: 40–45 MINS**

INGREDIENTS

2 tbsp olive oil

100 g/3½ oz chorizo sausages, skinned and sliced

1 onion, finely chopped

1 red pepper, deseeded and roughly chopped

400 g/14 oz boneless, skinless chicken thighs, cut into bite-sized pieces

4 large garlic cloves, finely chopped

350 g/12 oz paella rice

150 g/5½ oz frozen peas

1 tsp Spanish sweet paprika

large pinch of saffron threads

125 ml/4 fl oz dry white wine

700 ml/1¼ pints chicken stock or vegetable stock

200 g/7 oz large raw prawns, peeled and deveined

salt and pepper

chopped fresh flat-leaf parsley, to garnish

lemon wedges, to serve

1. Preheat the oven to 220°C/425°F/Gas Mark 7. Heat the oil in a flameproof casserole over a high heat. Reduce the heat to low–medium, add the chorizo and fry, stirring, for 3–4 minutes until it starts to brown and gives off its oil. Remove from the pan and pour off all but 2 tablespoons of the oil.

2. Add the onion and red pepper and fry, stirring, for 3–5 minutes until soft. Add the chicken and garlic and stir until the chicken is coloured all over.

3. Add the rice and peas, gently stirring until the rice is coated in oil. Stir in the paprika and saffron threads, then add the wine and stock and season with salt and pepper. Bring to the boil, stirring occasionally, then transfer to the preheated oven and bake, uncovered, for 15 minutes.

4. Remove from the oven and add the prawns and chorizo, pushing them down into the rice. Return to the oven and bake for a further 10 minutes, or until the rice is tender, the prawns are pink and cooked through and the chicken is done. Cut into the middle of the chicken to check there are no remaining traces of pink or red. Garnish with parsley and serve with lemon wedges.

JAMBALAYA

SERVES: 4 **PREP TIME: 25 MINS** **COOK TIME: APPROX. 45 MINS**

INGREDIENTS

2 tbsp vegetable oil

2 onions, roughly chopped

1 green pepper, deseeded and roughly chopped

2 celery sticks, roughly chopped

3 garlic cloves, finely chopped

2 tsp paprika

300 g/10½ oz skinless, boneless chicken breasts, chopped

100 g/3½ oz kabanos sausages, chopped

3 tomatoes, peeled and chopped

450 g/1 lb long-grain rice

850 ml/1½ pints chicken stock or fish stock

1 tsp dried oregano

2 bay leaves

12 large raw prawns, peeled and deveined

4 spring onions, finely chopped

salt and pepper

chopped fresh flat-leaf parsley, to garnish

1. Heat the oil in a large frying pan over a low heat. Add the onions, green pepper, celery and garlic and cook for 8–10 minutes, until all the vegetables have softened. Stir in the paprika and cook for a further 30 seconds. Add the chicken and sausages and cook for 8–10 minutes, until lightly browned. Add the tomatoes and cook for 2–3 minutes, until they have collapsed.

2. Add the rice to the pan and stir well. Pour in the stock, oregano and bay leaves and stir well. Cover and simmer for 10 minutes.

3. Add the prawns and stir. Re-cover and cook for a further 6–8 minutes, until the rice is tender and the chicken and prawns are cooked through.

4. Stir in the spring onions and season to taste with salt and pepper. Remove and discard the bay leaves, garnish with parsley and serve immediately.

CHICKEN CASSEROLE WITH A HERB CRUST

SERVES: 4　　　**PREP TIME: 15 MINS**　　　**COOK TIME: 1 HR 40 MINS**

INGREDIENTS

- 4 chicken legs
- 2 tbsp plain flour
- 15 g/½ oz butter
- 1 tbsp olive oil
- 1 onion, chopped
- 3 garlic cloves, sliced
- 4 parsnips, cut into large chunks
- 150 ml/5 fl oz dry white wine
- 850 ml/1½ pints chicken stock
- 3 leeks, white parts only, sliced
- 75 g/2¾ oz prunes, halved (optional)
- 1 tbsp English mustard
- 1 bouquet garni
- 100 g/3½ oz fresh breadcrumbs
- 75 g/2¾ oz Caerphilly cheese, crumbled
- 50 g/1¾ oz mixed fresh tarragon and flat-leaf parsley, chopped
- salt and pepper

1. Preheat the oven to 180°C/350°F/Gas Mark 4. Toss the chicken legs in the flour, shaking off any excess. Melt the butter with the oil in a flameproof casserole. Add the chicken and fry, turning occasionally, until golden brown all over. Remove with a slotted spoon and keep warm.

2. Add the onion, garlic and parsnips to the casserole and cook for 20 minutes, or until the mixture is golden brown.

3. Add the wine, stock, leeks, prunes (if using), mustard and bouquet garni and season to taste with salt and pepper.

4. Return the chicken to the casserole, cover and cook in the preheated oven for 1 hour. Meanwhile, mix together the breadcrumbs, cheese and herbs.

5. Remove the casserole from the oven and increase the temperature to 200°C/400°F/Gas Mark 6.

6. Remove the lid of the casserole and sprinkle over the crust mixture. Return the casserole to the oven, uncovered, for 10 minutes, until the crust starts to brown slightly, the chicken is cooked through and the juices run clear when a skewer is inserted into the thickest part of the meat. Serve immediately.

SWEET CHILLI CHICKEN WITH CREOLE RICE

SERVES: 4

PREP TIME: 15 MINS PLUS MARINATING

COOK TIME: APPROX. 45 MINS

INGREDIENTS

8 skinless, boneless chicken thighs, about 100 g/3½ oz each
2 tbsp sweet chilli sauce
2 tbsp orange juice
2 garlic cloves, crushed
salt and pepper

CREOLE RICE

600 ml/1 pint water
250 g/9 oz long-grain rice
1 tbsp olive oil
1 large red pepper, deseeded and finely chopped
1 small onion, finely chopped
1 tsp paprika
400 g/14 oz canned mixed beans, drained and rinsed

1. Put the chicken thighs in a shallow non-metallic bowl. Mix together the chilli sauce, orange juice, garlic and a little salt and pepper in a small bowl and spoon over the chicken. Turn the chicken to coat thoroughly in the marinade. Cover and leave to marinate in the refrigerator for 1–2 hours.

2. Preheat the oven to 180°C/350°F/Gas Mark 4. Transfer the chicken thighs to a non-stick baking sheet and bake in the preheated oven, turning halfway through, for 25 minutes, or until tender and the juices run clear when a skewer is inserted into the thickest part of the meat.

3. Meanwhile, make the creole rice. Pour the water into a saucepan, add a little salt and bring to the boil. Add the rice and stir well. Cover, reduce the heat to low and leave to simmer, undisturbed, for 15 minutes, or until tender.

4. Heat the oil in a pan over a medium–high heat, add the red pepper and onion, and cook, stirring frequently, for 10–15 minutes, until the onion is soft, adding the paprika in the last 5 minutes of the cooking time. Stir in the beans and cook for a further minute.

5. Stir the bean mixture into the cooked rice. Transfer to plates and top with the chicken. Serve immediately.

CHICKEN WITH FORTY CLOVES OF GARLIC

SERVES: 6   **PREP TIME: 10 MINS**   **COOK TIME: 1½–1¾ HRS**

INGREDIENTS

1 chicken, weighing
1.6 kg/3 lb 8 oz

3 garlic bulbs, separated into
cloves but unpeeled

6 fresh thyme sprigs

2 fresh tarragon sprigs

2 bay leaves

300 ml/10 fl oz dry white wine

salt and pepper

1. Preheat the oven to 180°C/350°F/Gas Mark 4. Season the chicken inside and out with salt and pepper, then truss with kitchen string. Place on a rack in a casserole and arrange the garlic and herbs around it.

2. Pour the wine over the chicken and cover with a tight-fitting lid. Cook in the preheated oven for 1½–1¾ hours, or until the chicken is tender and the juices run clear when a skewer is inserted into the thickest part of the meat.

3. Remove and discard the bay leaves. Transfer the chicken and garlic to a dish and keep warm. Strain the cooking juices into a jug. Skim off any fat on the surface of the cooking juices.

4. Carve the chicken and transfer to serving plates with the garlic. Spoon over a little of the cooking juices and serve immediately.

HERO TIPS

If you find that the garlic is browning much quicker than the chicken, simply remove from the dish with a slotted spoon and set aside. You can then add them back into the dish a short while before the chicken is ready, to warm back through.

INDEX